D1716960

Tricky Insects
and Other Fun Creatures

by Rebecca Weber

Content and Reading Adviser: Mary Beth Fletcher, Ed.D.
Educational Consultant/Reading Specialist
The Carroll School, Lincoln, Massachusetts

Spyglass
BOOKS

COMPASS POINT BOOKS

Minneapolis, Minnesota

Compass Point Books
3722 West 50th Street, #115
Minneapolis, MN 55410

Visit Compass Point Books on the Internet at *www.compasspointbooks.com*
or e-mail your request to *custserv@compasspointbooks.com*

Photographs ©: Brand X Pictures, 5 (snail); all other photos courtesy of
Two Coyotes Studio/Mary Walker Foley.

Project Manager: Rebecca Weber McEwen
Editor: Heidi Schoof
Photo Selectors: Rebecca Weber McEwen and Heidi Schoof
Designer: Jaime Martens
Illustrator: Anna-Maria Crum

Library of Congress Cataloging-in-Publication Data

Weber, Rebecca.
  Tricky insects: and other fun creatures / by Rebecca Weber.
      p. cm. — (Spyglass books)
Summary: Provides directions for simple activities to learn more about
various common insects, snails, and worms.
Includes bibliographical references.
  ISBN 0-7565-0388-4 (hardcover)
  1. Insects—Juvenile literature. 2. Snails—Juvenile literature.
  3. Worms—Juvenile literature. [1. Insects. 2. Snails. 3. Worms.] I. Title.
  II. Series.
  QL467.2 .W375 2002
  595.7—dc21

                                     2002002756

© 2003 by Compass Point Books
All rights reserved. No part of this book may be reproduced without written permission from the
publisher. The publisher takes no responsibility for the use of any of the materials or methods
described in this book, nor for the products thereof.
Printed in the United States of America.

Contents

Insects All Around

From the busiest city to the driest desert, there are **_insects_** and other fun creatures going about their daily lives.

In the city

You can learn about the small animals that live near you. Just remember to always put the animals back where you found them.

In the desert

Moth Dance

On warm summer nights, you can find moths near lightbulbs. They like the warmth. They find food there.

At night, you can watch moths dance.

1. Hang up a sheet.

2. Shine a flashlight on it.

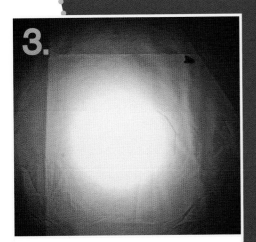

3. Soon moths will come to the light.

4. Watch the moths dance on the light.

Bug Motels

Many bugs hide in dark and shady places. This protects them from the sun. This also keeps them from getting too dry.

You can build your own bug motel.

Put a bowl in a hole.

Put in some fruit or meat.

Put a rock over the bowl.

The next day, see who stayed at the bug motel.

Snail Caves

Snails are always looking for food or a cool place to rest.

You can find out what they like best by building three different snail caves.

Make a cave
with five rocks.

Set out half
a grapefruit
and a bowl.

Leave the
caves overnight.

Which cave
did the snails
like best?

Slug Slide

Everywhere a *slug* travels, it leaves a sticky trail to slide across rough or dry places.

You can watch a slug use its slime to slide along.

Catch a slug.

Put it on
a glass plate.

Watch how
the slug
moves.

Look at the
slimy slug slide.

13

Worm Charms

Rain keeps dirt wet so worms don't dry out. Too much rain can drown worms.

You can *charm* worms by pretending to be a rainstorm. The worms will think the sound of the music is the rain falling.

Make some holes with a pencil.

Play music near the holes.

Watch the grass carefully.

Watch the worms come out.

15

Cricket Thermometers

If you are ever wondering what the **temperature** is outside on a warm summer night, just listen to the crickets. Crickets chirp more when it is warmer.

You can make a cricket **thermometer.**

Catch a cricket.

Count how many times it chirps in 15 seconds.

Add 40 to that number.

This number is the *Fahrenheit* temperature.

17

Butterfly Breakfast

Butterflies love to eat sweet-tasting food.

Invite some butterflies to breakfast by setting out some sweet food for them to enjoy.

Set out some fruit.

Set out some red sugar water.

Set out some flowers.

What do butterflies like best?

19

Fun Facts

When a baby spider hatches, it already knows how to weave a perfect web.

Some caterpillars eat close to their own weight each day. If you did that, you would have to eat nearly 250 peanut butter and jelly sandwiches every day!

A tiny flea can jump more than 300 times the length of its body. If you could do that, you could leap over three football fields, all lined up!

An **African** spider escapes danger by curling its legs into a wheel and rolling away.

Glossary

African–when something or someone comes from Africa

charm–to get an animal to do something by playing music

Fahrenheit–one way to measure temperature

insect–a small, six-legged animal

slug–a small, slimy animal that looks like a snail with no shell

temperature–tells how hot or cold something is

thermometer–a tool that measures how hot or cold something is

Books

Dussling, Jennifer. *Bugs! Bugs! Bugs!*
New York: DK Publishing, 1998.

Hartley, Karen, Chris Macro, and
Philip Taylor. *Flea.* Chicago:
Heinemann Library, 2000.

Wilkinson, Valerie. *Flies Are Fascinating.*
Chicago: Childrens Press, 1994.

Web Sites

www.uky.edu/Agriculture/Entomology/
ythfacts/entyouth.htm

yucky.kids.discovery.com/flash/roaches/
index.html

Index

GR: I
Word Count: 243

From Rebecca Weber

I grew up in the country, so I have always loved nature. I enjoy teaching people about the world and how to take care of it.